APOLLO PROGRAM

A BRIEF HISTORY FROM BEGINNING TO END

HISTORY HUB

Bonus Downloads

Get Free Books with __Any Purchase__History Hub

Every purchase comes with a FREE download!

Apollo Program

A Brief History from Beginning to the End

History Hub

© 2022 Copyright by History Hub. All Rights Reserved.

Please Note: The book you are about to enjoy is an analytical review meant for educational and entertainment purposes as an unofficial companion. If you have not yet read the original work, please do before purchasing this copy.

Disclaimer & Terms of Use: No part of this publication may be reproduced or retransmitted, electronic or mechanical, without the written permission of the publisher. The information in this book is meant for educational and entertainment purposes only and the publisher and author make no representations or warranties with respect to the accuracy or completeness of these contents and disclaim all warranties such as warranties of fitness for a particular purpose. Product names, logos, brands, and other trademarks featured or referred to within this publication are the property of their respective trademark holders and are not affiliated with this publication. This is an unofficial summary and analytical review meant for educational and entertainment purposes only and has not been authorized, approved, licensed, or endorsed by the original book's author or publisher and any of their licensees or affiliates.

CONTENTS

Chapter One: Introduction

Chapter Two: The Moon

Chapter Three: Why the Moon?

Chapter Four: NASA and the Competition between the U.S.S.R

Chapter Five: The Apollo Program

Chapter Six: Historical Perspective

Chapter Seven: To The Moon

Chapter Eight: Equipment, Systems, and Safety Nets

Chapter Nine: Struggles

Chapter Ten: Discoveries

Chapter Eleven:The Apollo Missions

Chapter Twelve: Neil Armstrong

Chapter Thirteen: Apollo 11

Chapter Fourteen:Apollo 13

Chapter Fifteen:Apollo 4 and Apollo 8: The Other Notable Apollo Missions

Chapter Sixteen:The End of Apollo

Chapter Seventeen:The Legacy of Apollo

Chapter Eighteen: Conclusion

Chapter Nineteen: Discussion

Chapter Twenty: Quiz Question

Bibliography

Your Free Bonus Download

Chapter One
Introduction

"One small step for man, and one giant leap for mankind." Neil Armstrong said this famous quote as he set foot on the surface of the Moon. It was indeed a monumental achievement that man has accomplished. The Apollo Project opened doors to the different possibilities involving the Moon and its relation to Earth. Because of the Apollo Project, there have been discoveries on our Moon, and those discoveries led to a better understanding of the Moon.

Why the Moon in the first place? Why would NASA and the government of America allow the people to spend tons of dollars on this project? Is it simply for vanity and pride? The answer to that can be explained in two ways. The first way is through political means. During the Cold War, the USSR and the United States were in constant competition as to which country was stronger when it came to military weapons such as missiles. When the USSR brought out Sputnik, the Americans – particularly President John F. Kennedy, urged his country to beat the USSR – he urged them to do better, be better. And that is what they did: they conquered the challenge posed by President Kennedy and, at the same time, called out the USSR, saying that they were the superior one between the two. Another way to explain why the people agreed to push through with the Apollo Project is simply through the eyes of scientists. These people are as mystified about the Moon as everyone is. So, the chance to study the Moon in ways that they used to just dream of is now reachable and tangible. And who can resist having a way to accomplish your goals?

The importance of testing something or preparing for something cannot be stressed enough. There was testing the spacecraft itself, which is incredibly important. There was the testing of the different systems and modules in the aircraft.

There was the training the astronauts had to go through before even being considered to be part of the crew. And, of course, there was talk about where the launch point would be held. Besides the equipment, NASA also included safety nets inside the spacecraft just in case. Once all the preparations were made and done, all the astronauts had to think about now was the mission and that they should accomplish it. They made many discoveries during their flights.

Now, onto the Apollo Missions – there were more than just two. The Apollo Missions started with Apollo 4 and continued up until Apollo 18. The most famous Apollo Missions were Apollo 11 and Apollo 13. Apollo 11 was the pinnacle of the Apollo Project's success. Because of Apollo 11, the quote from earlier was said. Yes, Apollo 11 is the spacecraft that brought Neil Armstrong and Buzz Aldrin to the Moon. Then there was Apollo 13, which was almost the complete opposite of Apollo 11. Apollo 13, due to some engineering failure, was not able to complete its mission. The end of the Apollo project took a few months of deliberation. In the end, they believed we've got everything we could learn from the Moon. It was time to close it down, to make way for other projects and save huge amounts of money.

Finally, like all historical events, the Apollo Program may have ended. Still, as it existed, it created impacts on different constructs of the world. Even as it ended, the Apollo program's effects are still felt to this day. We could feel it in the politics of the world, in the technological and scientific aspects of studies, and we could feel it in the current expeditions made by others across the globe. The Apollo Program has indeed caused a ripple effect throughout this world's history until today.

The best place to start the discussion of the Apollo Program is simply the purpose of the Program - to figure out the mysteries of the Moon. Before delving into the different gadgets on the

Apollo aircraft, before jumping into how the Apollo Programs started, let us first talk about, or rather read about, the main subject of the Apollo Program: the Moon.

Chapter Two
The Moon

The moon is unique in its own way. Our solar system, the milky way, the sun, and the other nine planets that orbit around the sun contain a minimum of three dozen satellites. However, our Earth only has one orbiting around it, which is our moon. Another unique fact about our moon is that compared to the other "moons" of the other planets, it is unusually close to the Earth, which creates the Earth-Moon system or "double planet."

There are other unusual observations about the moon. For example, its movements are called an "elliptical orbit." Another observation of the Earth-Moon system is that the density (the number of materials within a specific volume) is based on that of water, meaning the moon's density is 3.34.

The Earth-Moon system intrigues astronomy scholars because of the moon's size in relation to the Earth. Usually, the planet measures approximately four times larger in diameter compared to its satellites, which again usually orbit their planet for roughly a month, and the average distance is 240,000 miles away. The Earth-Moon system is intriguing because they do not follow these usual statistics.

Chapter Three

Why the Moon?

Like most celestial bodies, the Moon's origin has not yet been agreed upon by different scholars. Modern speculation started with George Darwin, who hypothesized that the Moon was the first part of the earth and then fission happened, which means they were separated. There were other questions relating to the origin of the Moon. How old is the Moon? How was it formed, and what are the compositions of the Moon?

The question of the origin and age of the Moon has interested many scholars of astronomy for years – even centuries. In the 1960s, there were three general theories that came up. One would be that the Moon and the earth were formed almost simultaneously from the same galactic cloud of debris that surrounded the Sun. The other theory is that the Moon was separated from the earth by either tidal movements or the force of an impacting foreign body. And the last view is that the Moon was actually from another solar system. As it was pulled toward our Sun, our earth's gravitational pull forced it to orbit us instead.

People hoped the Apollo program would give sufficient answers to conclude about the Moon's origin. If the Moon weren't a primitive, undifferentiated, and homogenous body, the Moon's origin would have been figured out because of the Apollo program. However, it was not that easy. The Moon is divided into concentric zones of different chemical compositions and, based on its geological history, has hindered people from knowing its true origin.

People need to collect more data to know exactly what the Moon is. Since they already have the gravitational effects, shape, gravity, and moment of inertia of the Moon, they would need more geophysical surveys to figure out the Moon's heat flow, the Moon mantle thickness, and seismic velocity structure, as well as if it has a metallic core.

However, there is a side of the Moon that is a total mystery to everyone: the back side of the Moon, which is more commonly known as the "dark side" of the Moon. Still, astronomers say that is the wrong term for it. This side of the Moon has become the inspiration for a lot of science fiction writers over the years.

Another question about the Moon is the origin of its lunar crates, and scholars ask themselves If they are formed the way our volcanoes were formed or by small impacts of large foreign bodies and meteorites. This question has caused much debate within the community of scholars. Both hypotheses can be backed by any of the three theories of the origin of the Moon and have scientific evidence as well.

To be able to understand the Earth-Moon system, it is required to learn about the origin of each and every component of the solar system. However, as of now, that is not possible, but because of projects such as The Apollo Project, we've come a long way from not knowing much about our Moon to knowing a great deal more.

Chapter Four

NASA and the Competition between the U.S.S.R

NASA, which is short for the National Aeronautics and Space Administration, is an independent United States government agency established back in 1958 for the purpose of research and development of different ways to explore the entire outer space, mostly but not limited to the Earth's atmosphere and the milky way.

NASA is an organization that is composed of four main focuses. The first is Aeronautics Research, which is where they develop flight technologies. The second is Science, which deals with understanding the origin, structure, and evolution of the universe and our solar system. The third main focus is Space Technology which is all about the development of space science and exploration technologies (which is different from the first because this does not mean aviation technology). The last main focus is Human Exploration and Operations; this is where managing logistics and operations come into play.

NASA was built in response to the Union of the Soviet Socialist Republic (U.S.S.R.), which launched Sputnik in 1957. Sputnik was the first artificial satellite to orbit our Earth. However, the launch of Sputnik happened during the Cold War (the Soviet Union Versus the United States). During those several years, the two countries have been competing with each other in terms of developing new missiles that can carry nuclear weapons between places and continents.

When Sputnik launched, it gave the U.S.S.R. an advantage over its current competition. Once in space, Sputnik orbited the Earth once every 96 minutes. Because of this leap in scientific means, the United States was pushed by the determination to protect their country. However, on November 3, 1975, the U.S.S.R. made an even bigger leap in scientific revolutions; they were able to bring a dog to space!

The people from The National Advisory Committee of Aeronautics (N.A.C.A.) were absorbed into the new Government Agency and other government groups like the Army Ballistic Missile Agency (also known as the Redstone Arsenal) of Huntsville.

Even though Neil Armstrong was the first man on the moon, he was not the first man to enter outer space. That title belongs to Yuri Gagarin, a Soviet Cosmonaut who was able to orbit the Earth for 108 minutes. A little over three weeks, NASA replied to this action by launching Alan Shepard into space – not for orbiting but for suborbital trajectory, meaning he went into space but did not go all the way around. Hence, he only stayed in space for approximately 15 minutes.

Besides the first dog and human in space, the U.S.S.R. achieved other accomplishments before the United States. Thanks to Luna 2, they were the first to make a manufactured object to touch the surface of the moon in 1959. Then the U.S.S.R.

launched Luna 3, and less than four months after the first person to fly to outer space, they sent in another Soviet cosmonaut to orbit the Earth for a whole day. The U.S.S.R. also gave way to the first woman to travel space, Valentina Tereshkova, through the Vostok 6 mission.

During the leadership of John F. Kennedy, the creation of NASA was well on its way. President Kennedy and his administration proposed that the United States be known for being the first to set foot on the moon. This was declared by the end of the 1960s, and NASA started the Apollo Program for many reasons, including this declaration of President Kennedy. Neil Armstrong was the chosen one, the man who first set foot on the moon.

Chapter Five

The Apollo Program

On May 25, 1961, President John F. Kennedy motivated his country to make a human being the first to land on the moon before the decade ended. The sky scientists were not as excited as the geologists were. On September 24, 1961, NASA made an announcement that the Manned Spacecraft Center was to be established in Houston, Texas. It was not only a place for people to design, develop, evaluate and test newly made aircraft or gears but also it will be a training ground for astronauts and help manage their missions. They appointed Robert R. Gilruth as the head of the Space Task Group and the Director of this new center.

Joseph F. Shea, a systems engineer who facilitated the development of the inertial guidance system for the Titan intercontinental-range ballistic missile, was chosen by Dyer Brainerd Holmes to conclude the debate about how the Apollo project started and flew to the moon. On November 28, NASA announced that the North American Aviation of Downey, California, had been given a chance to develop the Apollo spacecraft. On December 21, Holmes formed a group called Manned Space Flight Management Council for its purpose was to set a policy for the planning of an operating space system. During the first meeting, this Council decided that the launch vehicle, known now as Saturn V, would help the dispatching of Apollo during its circumlunar mission.

Finally, on February 20, 1962, NASA was able to launch a man named John Glenn to orbit, manning an Atlas missile around the globe three times. And on November 7, NASA decided that the Grumman Aircraft Engineering Corporation at Bethpage, New York, would be honored to design and develop the Apollo Lunar Model. As the year 1962 came to an end, NASA was able to make all the decisions needed to appease Kennedy's challenge. They were finally ready to launch the Apollo Program.

Basically, the Apollo project was the largest and most intricate project the United States has ever had, which involved operating a space flight program. The goal of this project was for an American citizen to land on the moon and safely return back to earth. Besides being the first to land and explore the moon, another parameter of the mission was for the crew to orbit the earth for two weeks. Within these two weeks, the crew would practice handling the spacecraft and make scientific observations.

There are three compositions of the three-person Apollo spacecraft. The first is the command module. This was designed so that the three-person crew could work, eat and sleep without feeling the discomfort their suits might bring. Besides the life-support equipment, they also had windows, periscopes, controls, and instrument panels so that the crew would be able to navigate and pilot their aircraft properly.

The second composition is the service module. Here, it contained fuel and rockets to make the aircraft fly in and out of the lunar orbit and, if needed, to change their main course.

The last composition is the Lunar Excursion Model (LEM), which is also known as the "Bug." Its function is to carry two men from the lunar orbit to the moon's surface and back to the lunar orbit before returning to the parent aircraft.

There were three steps the Apollo project had to do to follow protocol. Step one is the command and service modules were launched into the earth's orbit. The astronauts stayed in space for two weeks before returning to Earth; this is where they were to practice and familiarize themselves with the aircraft.

The second step involved sending all three modules (the composition of the Apollo spacecraft) into the earth's orbit. The Bug made it possible to move the command and service modules around and place them near the Bug. The Airlocks opened and only two of the three-person crew climbed into the Bug.

The last step is where the main mission takes place. They landed and explored the moon.

Chapter Six
Historical Perspective

Again, the Apollo Program was one of the most expensive and ambitious projects ever made by the United States during a time of peace. Most of the scholars specializing in this subject see the Apollo Program as a competition between the United States and the USSR because of what happened in the Cold War. As much as the Cold War and the competition between these two countries were essential in making the Apollo Program, scholars believed that there were other factors that made the Apollo Program a reality- internal perspectives. It is important to know that the Apollo Program caught the awareness and excitement of the American people. The scholars thought of the Apollo Program to be a bubble borne from the ideas of a special interest group, which grew in size because of the positive feedback.

On May 25, 1961, the President of the United States, John F. Kennedy, challenged his country to land an American man on the Moon before the decade ended. On April 24, Vice President Lydon Johnson attended the Space Exploration Program Council meeting and further attested to Kennedy's challenge to their people. By the end of the meeting, they all agreed to take up their President's request and challenge. On July 20, Congress provided them with a space budget 60% higher than Dwight D. Eisenhower (the President before Kennedy) requested. Because of the support they got from the government, by July 16, 1969, Apollo 11 launched from Cape Kennedy (now known as Cape Canaveral) In Florida. And three days after that, Neil Armstrong was the first man to step on the Moon's surface, with Edwin E. Aldrin Jr following 19 minutes right after him.

The reason behind the people's involvement and excitement to bring their own men out into space can be explained in three points. The first was the need for scientists to develop science and technology, fueled by their own scientific curiosity and ambition. The second point is purely political reasons; the

United States and the USSR were still in competition for military supremacy and competitiveness in their space endeavors. And finally, the last point is that the space technology and space research done during this time had two purposes: to end the competition peacefully and contribute to their military.

This is a picture of the Moon from NASA's archives.

This is President Kennedy giving a speech urging his people to support the Apollo Mission.

Are You Enjoying Reading?

As an independent publisher

with a tiny marketing budget

we rely on readers, like you.

If you're receiving help from this book,

would you please take a moment to write a brief review?

We really appreciate it.

Chapter Seven
To The Moon

Launch Site

When word got out that NASA was looking for launch sites, a group of Georgian businessmen suggested the coastal islands from their state. The team that handled the scouting for places made an ocular of the Cucumber Island and found that it had many advantages: it was undeveloped land, had railroad facilities, a coastal waterway, and port facilities. By the end, the team made a consensus that Cucumber Island would go under further study if it could really be the best place for the launch site.

Cucumber Island is 32 kilometers long, and the width varies, but its widest point is 5 kilometers. It has extensive tidal flats and many saltwater marshes, and the Intracoastal Waterway separates the island from Georgia's mainland; it also gives affordable access to water transportation. Also, King's Bay Ammunition Facility was near enough to provide accessible railroad sidings.

While the study of Cucumber Island was happening, they were able to acquire Cape Canaveral at around 10 million dollars. The Canaveral area has many overwhelming advantages. It was placed at the head of the Atlantic Missile Range, a series of tracking stations almost 9,000 kilometers, reaching Ascension Island. It was a training ground for the personnel to practice launching missiles. No big cities were close enough to be a hazard, and the noise will not disturb any civilian town.

By the month of July, the NASA Air Force has eight sites they are considering for the launch site. These sites are Cape Canaveral, Offshore from Cape Canaveral, Mayaguana Island in the Bahamas, Cucumber Island in Georgia, a Mainland site near

Brownsville of Texas, White Sands Missile Range in New Mexico, Christmas Island in the mid-Pacific south of Hawaii, and South Point on the Island of Hawaii. However, the two main places they are considering are Cucumber Island and Cape Canaveral.

These two sites share some advantages, such as accessibility to deep water transport, there are railroads, and there is no problem with overflight or booster impact. However, after further study, they found some issues at Cucumber Island: there is an interference with the Intracoastal Waterway, it would be an expensive launch area, land-based equipment for the early portion of the flight would not be available, there would be a need for downrange stations, there are small towns in the area as well, and finally the land area had too many primarily marshlands.

While there are six reasons why Cucumber Island won't be a good fit, Cape Canaveral has only two disadvantages: the land is comparatively expensive, and the cost of electrical power and hydropower is too high. In the end, they decided to create the launch site at Cape Canaveral, also known as Cape Kennedy.

Chapter Eight

Equipment, Systems, and Safety Nets

The heart of the system in any spacecraft is the flight computer – in our case, it's called the Apollo flight computer. It handles a great amount of different computational problems at the same time in real time. Also, it has a number of signal interfaces that can communicate with other systems in the aircraft. The use of this computer during flight experience shows the importance of error detection and built-in alarms in the hardware and software programs and the memory protection of these features.

The use of the digital computer to bring together the system's measurement processing and commanding functions has proven that the design is flexible. The computer program changes are not taken lightly and can be dangerous without retesting the new code. However, in most cases, changing the program to accommodate hardware problems has saved time, effort, and money expense.

An important phase of the Apollo mission is the rendezvous point of the Lunar Excursion Modules and the Control and System Modules, which follow the Lunar Excursion Module's ascent from the Lunar surface. However, the problem they've encountered is getting the exact measurements of the positions and the velocities of the two spacecraft. The concentric flight plan was made to provide a backup for astronauts using a simple onboard chart solution by the tracking calculations just in case the primary system goes down.

As a safety net, the control on the Apollo spacecraft has an autopilot feature. The initial trial of these autopilot designs was just a simple analog system approach. However, in 1964, NASA made a wise decision to incorporate the autopilot system into the Command Module and Lunar Excursion Module digital computers. All different configurations' autopilots in the digital computers were tested, and they all successfully passed. Because of the capabilities of the digital computer, it became possible and effective to program the scheduling of the auto-pilot system.

Chapter Nine

Struggles

NASA faced plenty of challenges as it prepared for its launch. One of the most obvious reasons that caused the difficulties in rocketry is the extreme volatility of the fluid and solid propellants. Besides the hazards of handling exotic and explosive materials, the combustion of the materials had to be contained but still powerful. Because of this, the engineers had to create a way where this explosive power could be channeled in a way that the heat and force would neither explode nor melt the combustion chamber or its nozzle. Rocket engineers then tried to learn how to cool the walls of the combustion chamber and nozzle; what they did to achieve this was to maintain the flow of the volatile liquids near the chamber and nozzle to redirect excess heat. Also, they implemented a strict cleanliness policy to make sure that the system they made would not be compromised.

For the solid fuels, it was important to match the shape of the solid fuel to the shape of the combustion chamber. After much research, the engineers were able to figure out the appropriate engine geometry for it to work and be contained.

The aircraft designers acknowledge that rocket engines create serious structural vibrations, making them aware that jet engines have a similar problem. Rocket engines are much more problematic compared to aircraft engines because their vibrations from the propellers are large and occur much more frequently. This then causes breakage of structural joints and mechanical connections of the different electrical equipment; it would be challenging to fly sensitive electrical equipment like vacuum tubes, radio receivers, and guidance systems. The vibrations are caused by the fuel moving around in the almost empty tanks and fuel lines.

The problem with vibrations is not easily solved because the oscillation causes a domino effect, affecting the entire craft's electrical equipment and mechanical connections. Because of this system issue, in the 1950s, these sorts of problems paved the way for the development of a new discipline within the engineering disciplines. What was needed was the creation and evolution of social and technical methods. Eventually, the engineers solved this problem as well.

To solve most – if not all – problems, systems management came into play to solve the major technical issues of both rockets and spacecraft. Because of the intricacy of this system, coordination and communication were heavily needed; proper communication helped achieve better and more functional designs. In summary, the problems of the space environment, automation, and the volatility of rocket fuels paved the way for new social methods that stressed up-front planning, documentation, inspections, and testing.

System management is a mix of techniques that help balance the needs and concerns of scientists, engineers, military officers, and industrial managers. This management's territory also includes the extreme environments, danger, and automation of missile and space flight technologies. Because of the integration of this different problem, the development of it all was smooth and great.

Chapter Ten
Discoveries

Thanks to the Apollo Project, the Moon is not as mysterious to us as it was before. Thanks to the three laser reflectors left on the Moon by the Apollo astronauts and another placed by the Soviet Lunokhod 2 lander, these three laser reflectors act as a mirror. They are designed to get measurements of the Moon in relation to itself and the Earth. Because of this, we now know that the average distance between the Earth's center and the Moon's center is 239,000 miles or 385,484 kilometers. We also know that the Moon recedes the Earth at the rate of one and a half inches per year. Also, the Earth's year length varies by about one-thousandth of a second per year.

There was also the discovery of moonquakes, which happen several thousands of times in one year. There are three very different kinds of moonquakes: one is due to impacts, the second is due to artificial objects hitting its surface, and the third is due to internal movements within the Moon itself.

Another discovery made is about the Moon's surface, which seems to be covered with broken-up rocks and dust. These components of the lunar's surface came from the material that created the Moon's craters. The ragged debris part of the Moon's surface is called the "Regolith," while the smoother side is called "lunar soil."

The lunar soil has different layers that are identified through meteorite impacts. The sun has an effect on the lunar soil; by studying the results of the sun on the soil, it is now possible to investigate further the sun's behavior over time. Also, the lunar soils are composed mainly of pyroxene, plagioclase, and olivine.

This is an Apollo Guidance Computer (AGC) and Navigation System from the second Lunar.

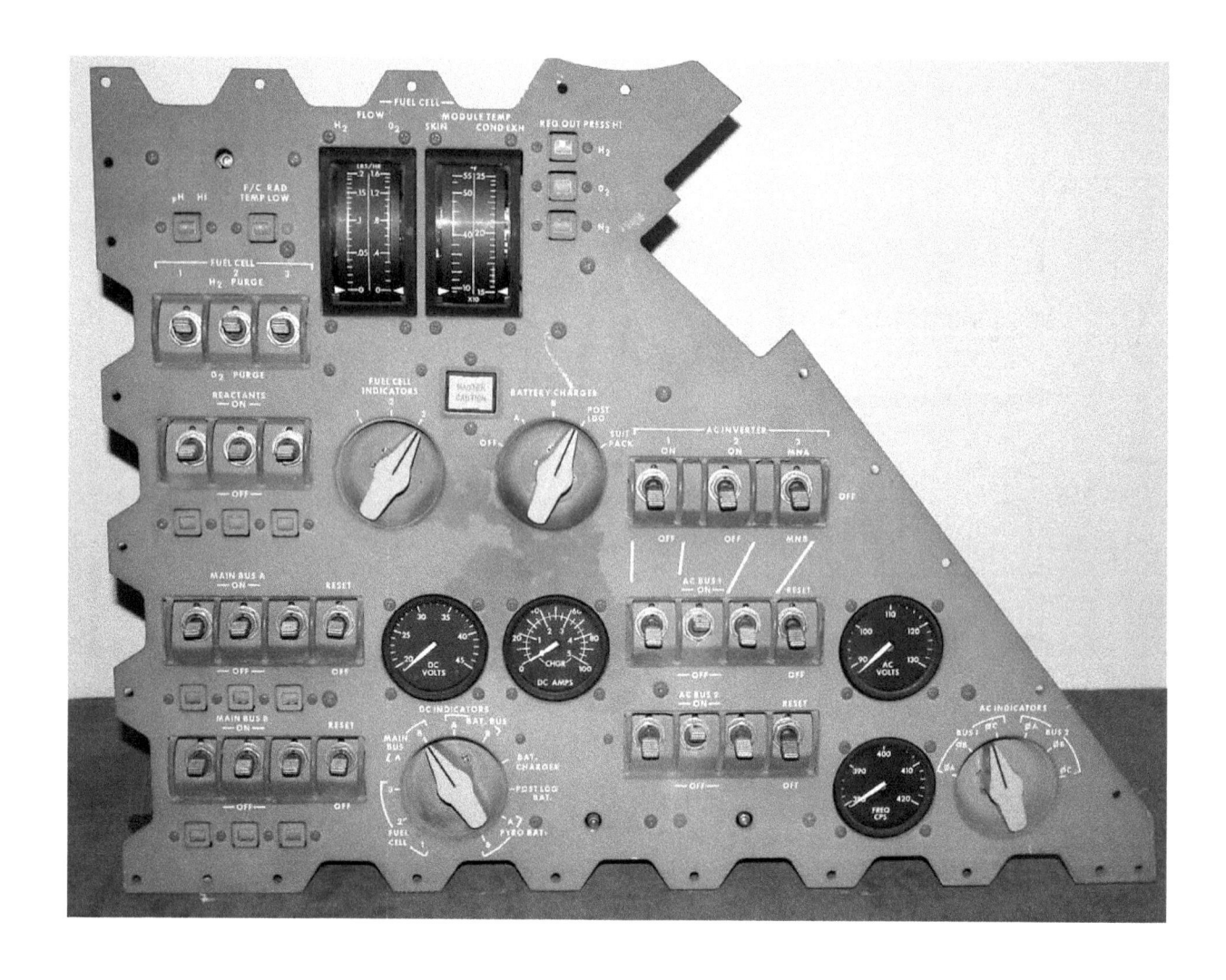

This is an example of Apollo's Command Module.

Chapter Eleven
The Apollo Missions

The Gemini Project and the Apollo Project

Like in any recruitment or team building, hiring the men who would take part in the Apollo project was a task; they needed to find people who had raw talent and potential to be able to make the mission a success. The US space program started this endeavor with military test pilots who became astronauts-in-training. Another characteristic that the Apollo astronauts shared is their educational and professional backgrounds in engineering. NASA wanted their astronauts trained in every aspect of the mission, including knowledge of the spacecraft in which they would be launched. Astronauts participated in the process of designing, building, and testing the Apollo aircraft. In Apollo 11, every astronaut had a specific role to play in their first mission.

Edwin Eugene Aldrin Jr, also known as Buzz Aldrin, was the face of NASA's solution to their challenges for the lunar mission. He was chosen to be part of the team because of his technical contributions to the new field of astronautics; also, he was part of the military. He was chosen mainly because of his Bachelor of Science in Mechanical Engineering and his doctorate in Astronautics from the Massachusetts Institute of Technology (MIT). These credentials are exactly what NASA was looking for.

NASA's move to include Aldrin in the team showed that NASA was ready for that mission to make it to the moon. Aldrin not only joined the team, but he also helped train astronauts to come aboard the spacecraft using the line-of-sight method. This method is not a "solo" method but a two-part act between the astronaut and the machine. Aldrin instructed the trainees to disregard their "intuitions as fighter pilots." He taught them to manually fly their spacecraft and land it on the moon even if there was no computer to help them.

The Gemini Program was the program before the Apollo Project and its competitor. Because of Aldrin, the Gemini project was successful. Its mission was to show that orbital docking between two spacecraft is achievable. Another assignment was to prove orbital rendezvous could be attempted and done right. Because it was orbiting the Earth, Gemini accomplished a mission that it wasn't expected; it almost made the Apollo program insignificant. Gemini was then referred to as "Mercury Mark II."

James Chamberlin soon combined Gemini with the Apollo program to take advantage of its success with the Saturn rocket. Gemini's plans never defeated Apollo's plan. Since the Apollo Program was a government project, it was superior. It was even considered to be the logical successor to the Manhattan Project. Now, they view Gemini as the trainer program that taught astronauts how to "fly in Earth-orbit."

Chapter Twelve

Neil Armstrong

Neil Armstrong graduated with a degree in aeronautical engineering and a Master's degree in aerospace engineering, which provided him with a strong impression of the US space program - he had significant potential for a great contribution to the program. He started by joining the National Advisory Council of Aeronautics (NACA) then he took his experiences gained from being the naval aviator at NASA's High-Speed Flight Station to the Dryden Flight Research Station, where he flew 200 models of different experimental aircraft over the Mojave Desert.

Even though his fellow astronauts thought he was the weakest link, Armstrong still became part of the astronaut corps in 1962 with several references and a large pool of experiences. Armstrong encountered a lot of mechanical challenges that made him think quickly and cleverly. His fellow men finally recognized his abilities as he solved each challenge with a cool head. He became the first man to walk on the moon.

Chapter Thirteen

Apollo 11

The three men who were launched to the Moon on July 16, 1969, on Apollo 11 were Armstrong, Aldrin, and Collins. Apollo 11 was the first event to be televised internationally through communication satellites. Since Armstrong and Aldrin were set to land on the Moon on the afternoon of July 20, it was delayed to the morning of July 21. President Nixon ordered all federal government offices to be closed, as well as other establishments, because of what was happening on that day, July 21. Nixon declared that day a national holiday to allow everyone to watch the first steps on the Moon without the stress of his people thinking about work.

Apollo 11 was on the dark side of the Moon when they told the station that they'd entered the Moon's orbit. As the crew looked out to the lunar surface, the crew admired what they saw. NASA requested them to describe the "landing path," and the crew told them about the craters, which made them realize that the topography of where they are looked similar elsewhere. However, they were able to find their bearings quickly.

Once they set their feet on the Moon, Armstrong said his most famous line, "That's one small step for a man, one giant leap for mankind." He also described the feel of the Lunar's surface to the Mission Operations Control Room (MCOR). Aldrin follows Armstrong right after. Of course, they still had their other points in the mission; Armstrong collected a moon sample just in case they had to abort the mission from unforeseen circumstances. Aldrin then focused on the collection of geologically important samples and documentation of the lunar surface exploration. Aldrin was able to capture three photos of Armstrong, creating proof that they were indeed on the Moon.

They also took seismic readings of the lunar surface and collected many pounds of rocks and samples. They also placed a plaque on the surface that said, "here men from the planet Earth set foot upon the Moon, July 1969, AD. We came in peace for all mankind." They landed on Earth on July 23, 1969, in the Pacific Ocean, where the men would be in quarantine for everyone's safety.

Apollo 11 accomplished its basic objective: for two men to land on the lunar surface and return safely to Earth.

Chapter Fourteen

Apollo 13

Although Apollo 11 is the most renowned space mission in history, it was not the only Apollo spacecraft that NASA launched. The next most famous one is Apollo 13. Right after Apollo 11, NASA scheduled the launch of Apollo 13 in March of 1970. But they needed more time to plan the expedition, so the launch was pushed back to April 11. All pre-launch operations ran smoothly during the winter months.

Something strange happened during the last day of testing back on March 25, 1970. The Graydon Corn's propellants crew started the cooldown of the LOX pumping system. The cooldown lasted for 40 minutes before the launch team emptied 39,000 liters of LOX into the drainage. Usually, the ocean's breeze makes the oxygen fog disappear, but this morning it didn't. The fog filled up the drainage ditch, and the invisible oxygen overflowed onto the bank.

The first person at the scene was Patrolman Nolan Watson. He walked to Earl Paige's car and overheard on the radio that a team was assembled to go to the wire bunker area. Paige then turned on his ignition, and flames appeared beneath the hood. Watson, in terror, ran back to his car only to find that it was also on fire. Thankfully, the fire was quickly controlled, and no one got hurt.

Apollo 13 was unsuccessful in its mission because it was shut down during the translunar flight because of the loss of all the oxygen stored in two tanks in the Service Module. This Apollo's missions were to perform a selenological inspection, survey, and sampling of the different materials in the preselected regions of the Fra Mauro formation. Another was to deploy and activate the Apollo lunar surface experiment package. The third was to develop man's capability further to work in lunar space. Finally, to take more photographs of potential exploration sites.

The crewmembers of the Apollo 13 were James A. Lovell, Jr., Fred W. Haise, Jr., John l. Swigert, Jr. Due to the prime Command

Module pilot coming in close contact with German measles eight days before the launch date, and it was revealed in his physical examination Swigert replaced him as a precautionary measure.

Chapter Fifteen

Apollo 4 and Apollo 8: The Other Notable Apollo Missions

Apollo 4 main objectives were to demonstrate the structural and thermal integrity and compatibility of the Saturn V and the mission's spacecraft. It also was supposed to verify the operation of the launch vehicle propulsion, guidance and control, and electrical systems. It also aimed to demonstrate the separation of the launch vehicle stages. It was supposed to prove the capability of the thermal protection system. Finally, it also aimed to show a service propulsion system engine with a no-ullage start.

Apollo 8 was the first launch that took men into the vicinity of the moon, which was a big leap forward toward the mission of achieving the Lunar Landing dream. Apollo 8 was also the first human-crewed mission to be launched with the Saturn V vehicle.

Chapter Sixteen
The End of Apollo

On August 5, NASA Administrator Paine wrote to John Findlay, the chairman of the Lunar and Planetary Mission Board (a NASA-chartered advisory group), to ask the board to create a review for the Apollo Project. The date of this meeting was August 24. Myers proposed to cancel Apollo 15 and Apollo 19 as he said they would save approximately 800 million dollars over time. Findlay, however, argued to both the Lunar and Planetary Mission Board and the Space Science Board that this project should not be shut down because "the loss of Apollo 15 from the program is serious, but the loss of Apollo 19 would be much more serious due to its capability for longer lunar surface EVA and its significant transverse capability." Basically, he's saying they would lose out on potential discoveries if they scrapped the project.

Bill Anders from the Space Council and Russ Drew from the Office of Science and Technology expressed their concern about Apollo 15 and Apollo 19 being canceled. Anders thought that if they stopped the project, there would be a hiatus of four years in human space flight, starting from the Skylab program to the space shuttle's first flight. Anders suggested that they should launch several earth-orbiting missions using the leftover Apollo spacecraft. NASA was about to make its decision, but a science adviser, Lee DuBridge, expressed his thoughts that the Apollo project would go to waste if they ended it now.

However, after this hearing, NASA's chosen course of action was to fly Apollo 14 in January of 1971, cancel Apollo 15 and Apollo 19, and rename Apollo 16 – 18 as Apollo 15, Apollo 16, and Apollo 17. Apollo 17 will now be the final lunar landing mission. They decided this action because it would save them money over time, and ending the Apollo missions would give way for them to focus on new projects.

This is an image of Apollo 11's lift-off.

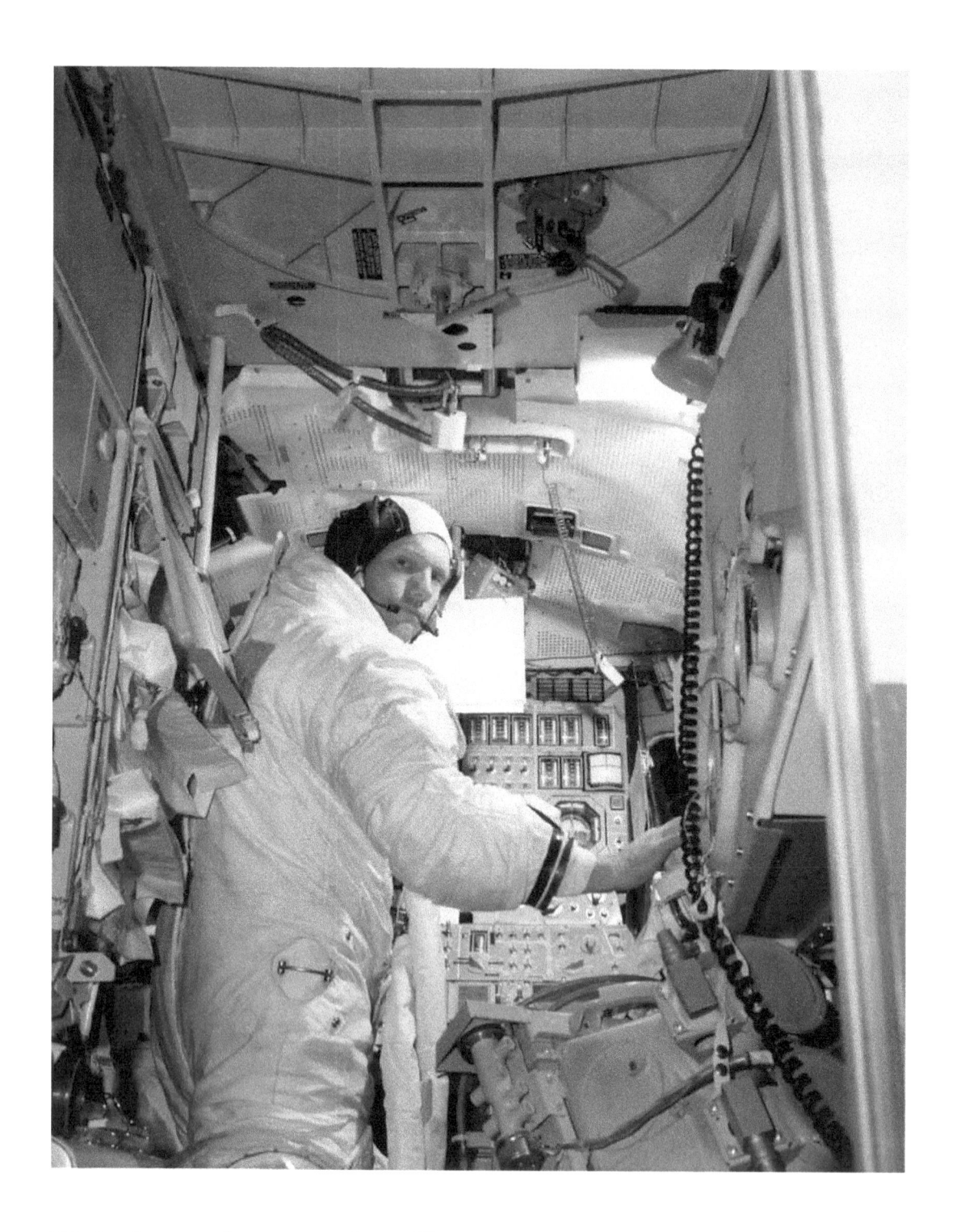

This is a picture of Neil Armstrong in Apollo 11's Command Module.

Chapter Seventeen
The Legacy of Apollo

The Apollo Project has left important impacts on our world today. The project established the technological fame the US had because of it. One of the many key success factors that the project had was its management model. Because of the Apollo Program, we now have 30000 photographs of the lunar surface that were taken during these Apollo missions. Also, because of its scientific nature, the astronauts on these Apollo missions were able to do biomedical experiments, leading to advances in medicine. Also, the Apollo missions started the advances in geology, human-crewed spaceflight, avionics, telecommunications, computing, math, astronomy, physics, bioscience, and other different technological and scientific constructs.

The Apollo program was nothing short of a turning point in history – not only in America but the entire world's history. The project showed both the technological and economic power of the United States. It also displayed its technological superiority over its rival state, named the USSR. The different effects the Apollo Project has touched upon can be divided into three parts: Political, Technological, and Exploration.

From a Political standpoint, Apollo became an important political symbol, serving as a unifying symbol in a troubled and pluralistic domestic state. It was internationally known to be the epitome of "prestige," which is a fundamental characteristic in international relations. However, a question remains: why would the United States undertake such a pricey project? What were its other benefits? One answer to this question could be that its benefits relating to the Cold War and the United States' interests outweighed the financial concern. Answer number two is about the political influence of technocratic groups.

These groups are connected to the military-industrial complex; therefore, they are usually influential in getting government resources for their programs – specifically the Apollo program. The third answer concerns itself with the particular role of Apollo as the political symbol. In this answer, Apollo is connected with the impacts on both national and foreign policies. This program played an important role in the Cold War. During the time of the competition between the United States and the USSR, the Apollo project met the important political needs that were essential to the United States' confrontation with the USSR.

One of NASA's missions was to use discoveries of science and technology from the space program to help strengthen the economic and educational systems of the United States. Through Apollo, space was able to be connected to the organization's importance to the modernization of Resources and Development. Another impact that Apollo had on the technological world is that it had an influence on the public's confidence in its own government's abilities.

When it comes to the Exploration effects that Apollo made, one of its most significant impacts is that Apollo was able to force people to view our Earth in a new way. The photographs from Apollo 8 and the other Apollo missions gave that to them. The images also made the people go into an environmental movement; the new outlook on our planet earth was that people now seemed to want to protect it and its life

This is a mural commemorating the first man on the moon.

Chapter Eighteen
Conclusion

If you feel empowered, that is a normal reaction to reading about the history of the Apollo Project. The beauty of this historical event is that it's borne from a challenge of the president and not out of revenge; a rare gem, a historical event that did not end in bloodshed. This proves that a momentous historical occasion can be more than just war and murder. Events like this, like the Apollo Program, prove to everyone that a "turning point event" can be a peaceful thing. You should learn from this that peace can be as loud, chaotic, and life-changing as violence.

Why would your professors always remind you to prepare for an upcoming test? Why do your parents tell you about an event, let's say for a wedding, beforehand? They do this because preparation is key. A lesson you must take with you as you end this reading is that practice is important. In the case of the Apollo Program, they had to pick the perfect location for their launch point. They investigated, tested, studied, and compared. All to make sure the launch point they choose is the perfect one. The Apollo crew was picked because of their backgrounds and knowledge. And since that was not enough, they also trained the crew. This is all in preparation for their take off to space. Why do they need to prepare? Because if they don't, they would not know what to expect or do on the mission itself. Think of it like you are taking your final exams. How will you know what to expect from the test if you do not study? How will you answer? How will you pass? Preparing for something is very important; if you don't, you will go into something blind, and that is not a feeling you would want to have.

Another lesson you must learn from the Apollo missions is testing. This is part of the preparation, but we must delve deeper into this. Testing is part of the scientific method. You must test your hypothesis to know whether it is correct or not. In the Apollo Program, they tested their equipment before you used it. Why should you test? The answer to this is simple: so when it is happening, you will have little to no problems. The point of testing something is to know if there are any problems and ensure everything is on point. Imagine if they did not test the spacecraft and found those errors during the mission. The repercussions would be great, that's for sure. So, testing is essential to life as well. For example, if you buy a phone charger, do you buy it without testing it in the store? Of course, you should because what if it has a defect? You will be wasting money and time. Testing is key.

In summary, you must always prepare for anything that comes your way so you do not go in blind. You must test equipment or other things to make sure they have no defects; it will save you time and money. And finally, you must remember that violence is not the only way for an event to become historical; peaceful events such as the Apollo Program are both historical and important.

Chapter Nineteen
Discussion Question

The two reasons why the Apollo project is because of what President Kennedy challenged and because of the scientific mysteries behind it. For you, what is the more important reason? Why is that your opinion?

Discussion Question

The competition between the United States and the U.S.S.R. during the Cold War is one of the reasons the Apollo Program came to be. The Apollo program was a response to their Sputnik launch. Do you think the Apollo Project was a response or more of a message that the United States is powerful? Why?

Discussion Question

NASA took its time in looking for the perfect launch site for the Apollo Project. They made a list and weighed out each pro and con of the location. Why do you think they were so meticulous in choosing the "perfect" launch point?

Discussion Question

Safety nets are always a good idea to have, especially for a mission as enormous as this. The Apollo Mission had an autopilot function as their safety net. If you were an engineer, what other safety nets would you install in the spacecraft? Why?

Discussion Question

Apollo 11's mission was successful, for it ended with all its tasks checked. In this mission, Neil Armstrong was the first one on the moon, followed closely by Buzz Aldrin. If you were Buzz Aldrin, how would you feel to be the second man on the moon and not have people talk about it as much as they talk about Armstrong's steps? After all, Buzz Aldrin did go on the moon, just a few minutes later than Armstrong.

Discussion Question

Due to some financial reasons, the Apollo Project had to be closed. They also said they had to shut it down to make way for more projects and because they believed they got enough of the information they could from the moon. Do you think these reasons are enough to close such a momentous project? What reason do you find not a good reason?

Discussion Question

The Apollo Project is a turning point in the whole world's history. Why do you think this mission affected the whole world when it was mostly the United States project? What about it makes it internationally relevant?

Discussion Question

The Apollo Program was made from competition, encouragement, and curiosity. If you were to create a new project for NASA, what would it be, and why would you suggest it? What significant effects in history do you think it would make?

Chapter Twenty
Quiz Question

1. **True/False:** The Apollo Project was born from three things. It was a response to Sputnik. It was a challenge from President Washington. And it was an interest to the scientists.

2. **True/False:** he Apollo Project's mission is to enter the Lunar orbit and land on its surface. The astronauts' tasks are collecting samples and taking pictures of the land. Part of the mission is to safely return to earth at a given time – based on their schedule.

3. **True/False:** Apollo 11 carried three men. Two of them were Neil Armstrong and Buzz Aldrin. The first man on the moon was Buzz Aldrin, who was followed closely by Neil Armstrong. Neil Armstrong set foot on the moon only minutes after Aldrin did.

4. **True/False:** pollo 13 was a success. Its engine held and completed its mission. The men part of this mission were James A. Lovell, Jr., Fred W. Haise, Jr., and John l. Swigert, Jr.

5. **True/ False**: NASA's primary choices for the launch site were Cape Canaveral and Cucumber Island. Both shared some advantages and had their own disadvantages. Ultimately, NASA chooses Cape Canaveral as the Launch site for the Apollo Program.

6. **True/False:** NASA chose people to be part of the crew based on their experience and their educational background. They also chose people who were part of the military and with engineering knowledge. This is because astronauts must know their way around the spacecraft.

7. **True/False:** The Apollo Project had more than just four missions. There were Apollo missions all the way to Apollo 20. It is just that Apollo 11 and 13 were the most notable ones.

8. **True/ False:** There are multiple reasons why the Apollo Project was shut down. One of the reasons is so that they can

save money over time. Another reason is that they wanted to make way for new programs.

Quiz Answer

1. False. It was a challenge from President Kennedy

2. True

3. False. Neil Armstrong was the first man on the moon, not Buzz Aldrin.

4. : False. Apollo 13 was not a success.

5. True

6. True

7. False. There were actually 18 Apollo missions, but it was edited to be called Apollo 17 instead. So there were only 17 Apollo Missions.

8. True

Bibliography

Images:

- "Full Moon - from NASA archive" by Ben Northern is licensed under CC BY-NC-ND 2.0. To view a copy of this license, visit https://creativecommons.org/licenses/by-nd-nc/2.0/jp/?ref=openverse.
- "President John F. Kennedy Urges Support for Moon Mission (NASA, Marshall, 05/25/61)" by NASA's Marshall Space Flight Center is licensed under CC BY-NC 2.0. To view a copy of this license, visit https://creativecommons.org/licenses/by-nc/2.0/?ref=openverse.
- "Apollo Guidance Computer (AGC) and Navigation System from the second Lunar Module, LM-2" by jurvetson is licensed under CC BY 2.0. To view a copy of this license, visit https://creativecommons.org/licenses/by/2.0/?ref=openverse.
- "Apollo Command Module Panel" by jurvetson is licensed under CC BY 2.0. To view a copy of this license, visit

https://creativecommons.org/licenses/by/2.0/?ref=openverse.
- "Apollo 11 Liftoff (NASA, Moon, 6/18/09)" by NASA's Marshall Space Flight Center is licensed under CC BY-NC-ND 2.0. To view a copy of this license, visit https://creativecommons.org/licenses/by-nd-nc/2.0/jp/?ref=openverse.
- "Neil Armstrong in the Lunar Module simulator" by Apollo Image Gallery is marked with Public Domain Mark 1.0. To view the terms, visit https://creativecommons.org/publicdomain/mark/1.0/?ref=openverse.
- "Apollo XI Man on Moon Mural" by Gary Lee Todd, Ph.D., is marked with CC0 1.0. To view the terms, visit https://creativecommons.org/publicdomain/zero/1.0/?ref=openverse.

References:
- Articles:
- Sheehan, T. (1975). Apollo Program Summary Report. *Houston, TX: National Aeronautics and Space Administration.*

- Kuittinen, H., &Velte, D. (2018). Mission-oriented R&I policies: In-depth case studies. *Case Study Report Energiewende. European Commission.*
- Gisler, M., &Sornette, D. (2008). Exuberant innovations: The Apollo Program. *Society, 46*(1), 55–68. https://doi.org/10.1007/s12115-008-9163-8
- Sadeh, E. (2006). Societal impacts of the Apollo Program. *Department of Space Studies. University of North Dakota, 20.*
- Benson, C. D., &Faherty, W. B. (1978). *Moonport: A History of Apollo launch facilities and operations* (Vol. 4204). Scientific and Technical Information Office, National Aeronautics and Space Administration.

Books:

- Crow, L. W., & Hare, D. L. (1989). *Apollo 11: A teacher resource book commemorating the 20th anniversary of the Apollo 11 moon landing, 1969-1989.* International Council of Associations for Science Education.
- Hoag, D. G. (1969). *Apollo navigation, guidance, and control systems: a progress report* (pp. 1-29). MIT Instrumentation Laboratory.

- Charles River Editors. (n.d.). *The Apollo Program: The History and Legacy of America's Most Famous Space Missions.*
- Harland, D. M. (2009). The Apollo zone. In *Paving the Way for Apollo 11* (pp. 203-285). Springer, New York, NY.
- Beattie, D. A. (2001). *Taking Science to the Moon: Lunar Experiments and the Apollo Program.* JHU Press.
- Johnson, S. B. (2006). *The secret of Apollo: Systems Management in American and European space programs.* JHU Press.
- Logsdon, J. M. (2015). *After Apollo?: Richard Nixon and the American Space Program.* Springer.
- Dick, S. J., Garber, S. J., & Odom, J. H. (2009). NASA HISTORY.
- Taylor, G. J., & Bays, B. G. (1994). *Exploring the Moon: A teacher's guide with activities for Earth and space sciences.* National Aeronautics and Space Administration, Office of Human Resources and Education, Office of Space Science.
- Heiken, G. H., Vaniman, D. T., & French, B. M. (1991). *Lunar Sourcebook, a user's guide to the Moon.*

Website:

- NASA. (n.d.). *Apollo Lunar Surface Journal.* NASA. Retrieved November 9, 2022, from https://www.hq.nasa.gov/alsj/
- Britannica, T. Editors of Encyclopaedia (2022, October 20). *National Aeronautics and Space Administration. Encyclopedia Britannica.* https://www.britannica.com/topic/NASA
- *The history of space exploration.* National Geographic Society. (n.d.). Retrieved November 9, 2022, from https://education.nationalgeographic.org/resource/history-space-exploration

Bonus Downloads

*Get Free Books with **Any Purchase**History Hub*

Every purchase comes with a FREE download!

Thank You For Reading

As an independent publisher

with a tiny marketing budget

we rely on readers, like you.

If you're receiving help from this book,

would you please take a moment to write a brief review?

We really appreciate it.

Milton Keynes UK
Ingram Content Group UK Ltd.
UKHW051838011224
451808UK00012B/189